HOUGH
NEIGHBORHOOD
LEGACY

*What We Had and
What We Lost*

GWEN GRAFFENREED

To order additional copies of this book, contact:
Xlibris
844-714-8691
www.Xlibris.com
Orders@Xlibris.com

ISBN: Softcover   978-1-6698-5874-4
         EBook   978-1-6698-5873-7

Print information available on the last page

Rev. date: 03/09/2023

Dedicated to the families of the community during this era.

Contents

Acknowledgments

Special thanks for Mr. Oliver & Mrs. Eliza Hough, Barbara McIntyre-Butler,

Shirley Gray, Ramona Menefee, Cynthia Felder, Brenda Webb,

Mount Sinai Hospital, Dr. Bruce T. Cohn, Cleveland Public Libraries,

Harvey Rice Library, Monika Anderson-Yates, The Donald Family,

The Haynes Family, Cleveland State University's Maxine Goodman Levin

College of Urban Affairs-Neighborhood Leadership Cleveland Institute,

Case Western Reserve University-Neighborhood Advisory Council,

The Legal Aid Society of Cleveland, Burten, Bell, Carr Development Inc.,

Famicos Foundation, City of Cleveland-Support Staff, Patricia Bowie,

Greater Cleveland Regional Transit Authority (RTA), League Park Recreation Center,

Cleveland Public Schools, Dunham Elementary School,

Addison Jr. High School, Ms. Holly, Brenda Webb, East High School, Principal Mr. Dinunzio,

Mr. Persky, Cynthia Felder, Thomas Edison School, Sandra Jones,

Xlibris, President John F. Kennedy, Dr. Martin L. King Jr., Senator Robert F. Kennedy,

Catholic Charities- Our Lady of Fatima Catholic Church, Dunham Christian Church, Bobbie Brooks, The Richmond Brothers, The Day Nursery Association,

Mrs. Utz, Mrs. Haffey, Mrs. Bracy, Pentecostal Church of God in Christ, and all the Foundations who sponsors neighborhood communities throughout Greater Cleveland.

Preface

The mental snapshot of growing up in Hough Neighborhood in the nineteen sixties during the *Civil Rights Movements, Hough Riots and Assassinations of World Leaders.*

There is an impulse in each of us to make in some manner, a very personal and individual mark on "our" neighborhood around where I we grew up in the latter part of the nineteen fifties. We moved Hough neighborhood on a street named Lexington Avenue in the Hough neighborhood. Lexington Avenue was such an interesting street in many ways.

In reminiscing it reminded me of a long decorative puzzle piece of a choo choo train. Starting at 55th street in Lexington Avenue ending at 79thon Lexington Avenue. Along the way you could observe large single- homes, tall/short brick apartment buildings consisting of first and second floors with four suites, League Park Center, Dunham Elementary School, Our Lady of Fatima Catholic Church, Night Club, Thomas Edison School Racetrack facing toward Lexington Avenue, Pentecostal Church of God in Christ, and Body Shop.

The sidewalks were well maintained. Which allowed residents to walk up and down the street safely. In those days, many families did not own multiple cars and walking was the way of life for some. Riding The Greater Cleveland Regional Authority (RTA) Hough Avenue bus number 38. Many residents rode the bus all the way downtown. To Cleveland Public Square, HealthCare Centers, Cleveland Public Library, going to work, school, shopping, to visit family members, and many more places.

Indeed, Hough was a working-class neighborhood, and many residents were employed. Throughout The City of Cleveland Communities/Neighborhoods and outside of city limits (Shaker Heights/ Warrensville Heights)

Although, times became difficulty our family members accepted the resources that the Government provided for qualified families. Many families appreciated receiving the long box of cheese, oatmeal, peanut butter, flour, pork & gravy, powder eggs and powder milk. Never observe anybody looking down on anyone because all of us were experiencing challenging times. We use too converse about cheese toast, and peanut butter sandwiches. Until we made up a song giggling and laughing about the block of cheese. Song: Cheese Toast Cheese Toast "yummy " for your tummy, tummy" .

Many extended families lived in Hough with male present in the household. It was noted as I was reading in many magazines and online articles. That in nineteen sixties Hough shifted to a majority Black population. Some ways it appeared that way, but it was not. However, many families came from southern states which were widely diverse. They were African Americans, Irish, Italians Europeans Latinos, Native Americans, and many more ethnic backgrounds.

The nineteen sixties brought triumph, tragedies, quality of education, observe changes in communities/ neighborhoods, 1966 Hough Riots, Glenville Riots, Vietnam War, and the assassination of three Great World Leaders President John F. Kennedy, Dr. Martin L. King Jr., and Senator Robert F. Kennedy.

Housing was one of the concerns for many residents due to extended families living in homes and apartments dwellings with two and three bedrooms. Many families became creative by turning dining rooms into sleeping spaces to accommodate the family and out of town quest.

I remember how the City of Cleveland employees would come around the neighborhood on Lexington Avenue and talking to the residents especially after the nineteen sixty-six Hough Riots.

I will always believe   It is Not Where You Live   It is How You Live

In this book " *Hough Neighborhood Legacy" "What We had and What We Lost* " I only will be writing about 1966 Hough Riots and the famous Lexington Avenue where I grew up, interacting with numerous activities in the community. I enjoy embracing diversity that the community offered.

I will continue to believe that our destiny is like puzzle pieces of life. We continue to add on and take away daily going through the journey of living. Too often we do not understand what is developing around us. Our lives are precious, and I have learned we will only be on this earth for a time. We should contribute are talents and every way we can.

We had the opportunity to reside through Elementary School, Junior High School, Senior High School in one living place (Resident) and many other families did as well. Thanks to our wonderful property owner Attorney James A. Haynes Jr. (African American). He was our family attorney and our family rented two suites in his four-suite apartment building. It was nice with two bedrooms with the dining room created into a bedroom. Many of families did that during those times for extra needed sleeping space.

Mr. Haynes did his own maintenance for his rental property and my stepdad assisted him when needed. They had a particularly good relationship. Mr. Haynes was a calm person with a pleasant smile and compassionate with all his tenants Whenever we fell behind on our rent. He always gave the family time to get caught up and we did.

During the summer months we would see Mr. Haynes more often to provide maintenances inside/outside of his nice rental apartment building. Especially, beginning of the Hough Riots I remember him calling talking to my stepdad and mom to see if we were all right. The other tenants received a telephone call as well. Mr. Haynes was not only the property owner, but he was our Attorney and friend.

The photograph of the apartment building is similar the one we lived in from
1960's (Elementary School, Junior High School and East High School)
Photo credit-The Cleveland Public Library

The History of Hough

**Hough Community is located on the Eastside
Cleveland, Ohio In Cuyahoga County**

The History of Hough and named after early settlers in 1799 property owners. Like many communities/ neighborhoods began as farmland and transition into modest neighborhood with fashionable homes. It was dedicated in 1873 and documented after last name of Mr. Oliver and Mrs. Liza Hough. The Hough community was named after it its major street. During those times it was attractable residential neighborhood surrounding large modern single homes.

Around the latter half of 1800's the emerge of development commercials institute businesses as Warner & Swasey Company and Hough Bakery 87th Hough. With well-established schools that served the elite families at that time. The early days around 1873 were Caucasian middle-class residents and shadowed by many wonderful establishments.

The two in mine is the University School located to Shaker Heights, Ohio. and the Cleveland Indians gradually moving to downtown Cleveland to Cleveland Municipal Stadium. Hough was documented as one of Cleveland oldest neighborhoods. Many wealthy well-known residents lived in Hough neighborhood in the early days. Around, the 1960's families began to transition from near downtown to Cleveland Neighborhoods from Orange Avenue, Central Avenue and Woodland Avenue to the Hough Community/Neighborhoods. To live in single homes and apartment buildings. It was a working-class environment., and many residents were employed.

The Year of Changes in The Neighborhood

Lexington Avenue

The name Lexington has many different meanings, one caught my eye can stand communication and entertainment theater and fun activities. I recall the most exciting actions occurred on Lexington Avenue. The Historic League Park Recreation Center was located at the corner of 66th street Lexington Avenue.

During summer months outdoor swimming pool brought much needed excitement. The pool was located facing more toward Linwood Avenue and very visible to see from Lexington Avenue. It was very much a popular attraction for young people coming from all over the community to join in on the fun of water play. I learned how to swim at League Park and was proud of myself.

Our family had settled into the Hough Neighborhood around 1950's . By, the 1960's I believe changes began to become noticeable due to the Great Migration. Many families moved into the neighborhood on Lexington and Hough Avenue as well as between side streets 73rd to 79th. Surrounding homes were large and few were changed into multi-family homes. Many families were homeowners. However, around Lexington Avenue especially on the side streets were plenty of tall and short brick apartment buildings. They were rental property and many of our friends and classmates lived in them. Due to the shortest of housing were occupied by of two or more children with extended family members.

I believe during the times our family moved into the Hough neighborhood on Lexington Avenue seemed to be friendly family environment with many family members living close around one another.

We had plenty of indoor and outdoor activities for recreations. Sponsored by the City of Cleveland,

Cleveland Public Schools, Dunham Elementary School, Addison Jr. High School, Our Lady of Fatima Catholic Church, and League Park Recreation Center.

I believe many residents in the communities/neighborhoods enjoyed coming to Thomas Edison Racetrack events to observe the excitement of the different area schools running against one another. Back in those days children seem to enjoy the excitement of fun and laughter.

After, the racetrack game was over. I remember sitting on the porch observing young people(around my age) walking past the apartment where we lived some talking softly and loud about the game. When walking down Lexington Avenue to home toward 79th street or to wait for the RTA buses.

I honestly believe having these types of programs Cleveland Public Schools demonstrated how they invested and believed in the Community/Neighborhoods.

Knowing many of the families were living in crowded household's conditions. Any type of recreation programs inside or outside was essential.

League Park Recreation Center

Lexington Avenue

It was built for the entertainment teams. I will name a few Cleveland Indians and Buckeye Negro American League.

Over, time like many communities/neighborhoods' transitions began and times changes for Institutions will not remain in declining neighborhoods for their economic stability. So, the Cleveland Indians had a space an opportunity in to move downtown to Cleveland Stadium. Around the 1950's City of Cleveland became the owner of League Park and turned it into Recreation Center well needed for the community/neighborhood.

One of the major attractions during the summertime was the outdoor swimming pool. It was always well attended by many community residents as well as out of the community. I remembered the Cleveland City Workers followed the safety rules with handwritten emergency forms to be completed by "our" parents. Our mom always or family member would usually accompany us during visiting outdoor swimming pool activities.

League Park Recreation Center has been instrumental providing afternoon space for residents who needed it. I was one of them who received support with enhancing my reading skills. When I was attending Dunham Elementary School the principal and teacher had requested for me Individual Educational Plan to enhance my reading skills . I was having difficulty comprehending important keywords to understand what I had read. Mom was instrumental in meeting with the young Caucasian lady from Western Reserve University.

She was not afraid to come into the Hough Neighborhood to give me tutoring lessons. We met at League Park Recreation Center in the evening. She took each page as I was reading and explained what keywords to look for in the beginning and the ending of the reading materials.

Once I completed tutoring classes and demonstrated my understanding. She was pleased with my accomplished as well as my mom. She gave me a 1960 Red Cover Webster Illustrated Dictionary to share with family and friends. Which I did and the dictionary is on my bookshelf to this day. The advance tutoring classes enhanced my reading skills. It became easier for me to understand what I read as I continue with my education through the years. Thanks to the Cleveland Public Schools principals and teachers for identifying Individual Educational Plan (IEP)for children who needed additional assistant in their physical, language, math, cognitive, social, emotional and creative developments.

Our Lady of Fatima Catholic Church

Lexington Avenue

According to my readings Bishop Edward F. Hoban established Our Lady of Fatima Catholic Church. In the month of November 27, 1949 about seventy-three years ago. To serve the Eastern Europeans . It was documented that the first Mass was held at the Thomas A. Edison Cleveland Public School. Until they were able to purchase the Italian Ritro Club, which was formerly Park Movie theater in 1950's and refashioned the building into a church for the neighborhood. Many original members began transitioning out of Hough neighborhood moving toward the suburb communities. Opening the doors for Puerto Rican immigrants who moved into the Hough neighborhood.

By the late 1950's more of the residents were African American with diverse family backgrounds. Their religious backgrounds varied according to families. Some residents I believe attended Baptist Church, Pentecostal Church of God in Christ, and Jehovah Witness Church etc.

I was baptized at an early age in the Catholic religion, and I remained in the faith my mom chose for me. During the years I lived in the Hough neighborhood I was a parishioner at Our Lady of Fatima Catholic Church. As I am reminiscing it is bringing on a smile with my head going up and down of my happy experiences with families and children who worship at the church. Church had *Fun Day Celebration* with variety activities. Many of my friends attended Fun Day with me and they were welcome with friendly smiles.

Our Lady of Fatima Catholic Church accepted all families and children in the community with open arms. The staff was very much diverse and blended into the community quite well.

Even though the Hough Riots lasted from (July 18 to 23) 1966) Our Lady of Fatima Catholic Church, Dunham Christian Church, and Pentecostal Church of God in Christ and many more churches were instrumental in supporting the residents, merchants, and the neighborhood.

During this senseless 1966 Hough Riots that changed the *Dynamics and Fabric of the neighborhood.* We had everything we needed during those times. Even though times were challenging but we learned how to survive and adjusted by working together as a family, neighbors, and friends. Together we did survive.

Cleveland Public Schools

In latter part of the 1960's Cleveland Public Schools in Hough community/neighborhood were going through a transitions period. It was documented a shortage of teachers and classrooms mostly on the city's East side of town in African American neighborhoods.

Our family adjusted to the many changes of the school system by becoming a member of the Parent Teacher Association (PTA).In 1960's The Ford Foundation funded a project at Addison Jr. High School to eliminate students' dropouts to strengthen educational skills.

This Funded Program was much needed for the families in the Hough neighborhood. Many of students who attended Addison Jr. High School graduated went on to East High School or another High School.

The Ford Foundation was very instrumental in assisting many students by encouraging us to stay in school and we did.

Cleveland Public School

Dunham Elementary
Lexington Avenue

I attended Dunham Elementary school in the Hough Neighborhood.

During those times children walked back and forward to school with their classmates. Occasionally, we had family members or neighbors to escorted us to school .

Dunham was a nice elementary school with memories of meeting new classmates and teachers. That is where I began engaging in developing relationships with peers and adults outside of family members. Meeting teachers and classmates was scary at first but as time went on, I became more relaxed in my school environment.

During my time at Dunham Elementary I developed a lifelong friendship with Lois; it continues through Addison Jr. High, East High School, and Cuyahoga Community College. We always took the time to call or send a greeting card to one another or met downtown for lunch, most important we stayed friends for over fifty years.

In elementary school we had many daily assignments. Reading and writing was incredibly important to my mom because long time ago people were not allowed to read or write. Since I had a long name (*Gwendolyn Graffenreed*) between my mom and teachers I had to spell my name, print, and write correctly with pride.

Looking back, I did not enjoy them repeatedly reminding of this task. Finally, I made sure and demonstrated that I accomplished what was expected of me. I came from a family of teachers who lived in the south, but mom was not a teacher but received guidance from them. Occasionally, she worked outside of the house. She was a homemaker and when Dunham Elementary School was overcrowded, we had half day sessions. She would be at home to care for us.

The family followed up with our education by reinforcing what we were learning in school. I remember my mom going to school with me to collaborate with the teachers to receive the upcoming assignments. So, she can follow up with us since we were going to school a half day.

Our maternal Uncle Will and Aunt Catherine(Teacher) and mom purchased a set of Orange Cover Childcraft Encyclopedia to provide home schooling. This was to encourage us to take our education seriously at an early age. Indeed, it did.

My mom brought me a *Small Red Plaid Book Bag* with handles. To put my school supplies and assignments in. Today I carry a briefcase to keep my papers from work and for meetings that reminded me of my book bag from childhood .

The memories of attending Dunham Elementary School that was located across the street from League Park Recreation Center and next to the school was a favorite delicatessen store. That sold French Fries inside a small white bag with ketchup. I remember many of our classmates enjoyed going into the store to purchases French fries and candy and I was one of them. The owner of the store was such a nice Caucasian man, and I can see his calm smiling face as I am typing this sentence.

I partially, enjoyed interacting in a diverse environment with teachers, classmates, and families in the neighborhood. Dunham Elementary School staff showed us how to embrace the love *of learning* at an early age with our parents.

Many of the teachers knew that they had a challenging responsibility working with the families in the Hough neighborhood. I can honestly say that they showed compassionate toward the families just listening to my mom telephone conversations with relatives.

My strongest memories how we were so blessed to have nice school staff during these times. We needed an environment that was enriching, and we were blessed.

Cleveland Public School

Addison Jr. High School
1725 East 79th Hough Avenue
Cleveland, Ohio 44103

In 1965, I graduated from Addison Jr. High School located facing East 79th Street and Hough Avenue. The times I attended was rewarding in so many ways.

Meeting new classmates and classmates from Dunham Elementary School continued to develop relationships. As a teenager as we were friendship was important growing up. Addison Jr. High School is where I learned the importance of having socialization outside of the family. Although, families are important, and friends are important as well. To develop friendships to strengthen relationships.

Addison Jr. High School was all about taking our education serious in the schools and out of the schools. This was the beginning process of growing up to become young respectable young adults in the community. I learned a lot about social development by interacting with peers and adults. In school by developing my talents I grew mentally, physically, and confidently. I give credit to our families, schools, community that provided such a good system/environment during 1960's with all the challenges all throughout the world.

Unfortunately, while sitting in the classroom at Addison Jr. High School. Our Irish President John F. Kennedy had been assassinated in Dallas, Texas and pronounced dead. I still mentally get flashbacks observing my classmates and teacher looking so stunned as well as me. Tears began running and dropping down from our faces on our clothing and desks. Crying became softly then loud with anger. You could never imagine the classroom environment atmosphere during those moments. I know my heart was just broken because President John F. Kennedy was the only one as president of United States of American that I truly was beginning to learn about politics. His speeches were just captivating to me.

To this day I have a photograph of him on the living room wall surrounded with Dr. Martin L. King Jr., Senator Robert F. Kennedy, and family photographs.

We had to learn to endure crises in our community and Crises in United States of America with our families and Cleveland Public School Staff.

My appreciation for our home room teacher Mrs. Holly (African American) who was firm and caring toward her students. She had a good repour with my mom and did not have any problem calling our house if any concerns arose.

Our beloved Principal Joseph Dinunzio was Italian, and he knew many of his students and parents. Many of the parents adored him because we used to listen and giggle to their comments and conversations about him being so handsome and approachable. Mr. Dinunzio and his diverse staff were positive role models for the Hough Neighborhood families and children.

Classmate: Addison Jr. High School

Long time friend Brenda Webb we met at Addison Jr. High School in Home Economic Class. She said to me while we were sitting down having lunch at Beachwood Mall " Gwen growing up in the Hough community shaped my character in many ways. The people we lived around were like family We took care of each other" It taught me to have compassionate for others and, also to strive to be the best at whatever I do" My close friendship with Brenda continues as of today.

Addison Junior High School
Cleveland 3, Ohio

CONGRATULATIONS

Gwendolyn Graffenreed

The faculty, staff and students of Addison Junior High School congratulate you upon completing the ninth grade. You carry our best wish for success in high school. We are grateful for the contributions that you have made to our school.

May you develop your talents and grow mentally, physically and morally strong and be a credit to your family, school, community, and to your country.

Home Room Teacher

June 16, 1965
Date

Joseph Dimbuzio
Principal

Addison Jr. High Diploma

Cleveland Public School

East High School
Blue Bombers

When I graduated from Addison Jr. High School and went on to East High School and Mr. Joseph Dinunzio again became our principal. My mom and many other parents and students were delighted when they heard that he would become our principal again.

In the 1960 East High School was very diverse in many ways. I was assigned to Mr. Persky homeroom who was Caucasian. As I am writing I can see him walking around (Aisles) checking attendance wearing his grey suit that complimented him quite well. He had a calm voice with a smile on his face as he interacted with his students. He gradually gained repour with his students and their parents.

The goals for us were to continue to develop our skills mentally, physically, socially, intellectually, emotionally, and creatively to enhance our talents.

One of my favorite classes at East High School was Home Economics. We had the opportunity to work in small groups to gain experience to make simple dishes as well as learn etiquette procedures. This class gave me more excitement in developing homemaking skills. First year attending East High School during the summer break. It was a sizzling summer night when the 1966 Hough Riots broke out on Hough Avenue.

Classmates : East High School

Long time friend Cynthia Felder sent me an email sharing her thought about living in Hough neighborhood. "It was like a well-oiled machine. People respected each other and their property. They also respected grocery stores,, churches, libraries hospitals, schools, and cleaners in the neighborhoods. Everything was available to serve everyone. Neighbors respected and cared for each other's. Outside forces created the Hough Riots by removing convenience in the area. People rebelled because they lost caring and sharing that neighborhood provided. I survived the Hough Riots and Glenville Riots because I refused to let it prevent me from reaching my goals in life." My close friendship with Cynthia continues as of today.

Dr. Martin L. King Jr. was assassinated on April 4, 1968

Just before we graduated from East High School. That was incredibly sad day for many families and children in the community. My whole family was very heartbroken hearing the news of "our" leader of nonviolence. His speeches were powerful to listen too. He brought of us hope and self-worth be the best you are in whatever you do. But be the best.

I finally passed all school requirements to graduate from East High School. Our graduation was in June 1968 held at Severance Hall since we had such a large class. After graduation it was time for us to begin "Our journey into the working world of life. Our families did their job in raising us, Cleveland Public School did their job in educating us and the City of Cleveland did their job by continuing supporting the neighborhoods.

(We made it because so many people believed in us besides our families)

Hough Riots

July 18-23, 1966

The Hough Riots happen during sizzling summer month in July 1966. When returning to East High School after the summer break . Still freshly in the air, news media., in newspapers and magazines. Showing National Guards patrolling the Hough Riots neighborhoods. I was a young teenager remembering the damages it caused our neighborhood.

The Hough riots sounded like a war zone like you would see in the movies. Hearing loud noises, bottle throwing, gun shots, sirens, loud voices, loud shouting, looting, and arsons, many houses, buildings and businesses. Were destroyed.

The Police did not have enough workforce to manage the out- of -control hostile crowd.

The mayor of Cleveland contacted the National Guards to assist the Cleveland Police Department to manage the out-of-control situation. It took some time to control this malicious planned riot. The RIOTERS demonstrated their characters of immaturity of how to solve problems. Unfortunately, we needed assistance, thanks to the mayor.

When the National Guards were patrolling Lexington Avenue. We were peeking through front window venetian blinds looking at them. As they were passing by the apartment, we were living in. We were instructed not to peek out the window anymore. That can bring danger to our home. Television was our entertainment and, we were told to stay quiet. We did follow the instructions what we were asked to do.

I remember being extremely nervous, crying, angry, and did not like staying in the house. I was tired staying in the house. It was summertime and it was time to visit Aunt Katie, friends and going shopping.

Hough Riots changed a vibrant neighborhood we thought was serving the needs of the community. Yes, we did have some problems with unemployment, and housing much more than I can imagine.

I realize that it was a lot of tension concerning Civil Rights Movement for Americans. We had wonderful community leaders, African Americans, Caucasian, Jewish, Italians, Irish, Puerto Ricans, Native Americans and many more nationalities. Great community leaders during 1960's who gave us hope, and sense of dignity, self-respect, and self-worth.

The Hough Riots was very senseless act tearing up your own neighborhood. It does not make any logical sense and it tells how the minds of the people who created this terrible act. Destroying a neighborhood that had much potential for growth. With beautiful historic well-built buildings and architectural set, up.

Since housing conditions was one of the concerns during the 1960's. Many families in the Hough Neighborhood had a lot of family members who had skills and skillful in carpentry, plumbing, electrical backgrounds, and painting could have assisted with property owners with repairs.

Just could have work with the property owners but all property owners were not slum property owners. There were African American property owners that took impressive care of their tenants and rental property quite well.

We must take in consideration that many of household were overcrowded, and it can cause many problems with maintaining rental property. We needed to be more mindful of home repairs if you must continue to repair the same problems. In plumbing and other major repairs due to overuse of equipment. When it is overcrowded and repeatedly repairing the same problem and it causes the property owner money.

The Hough Riots changed the whole fabric environment of a promising neighborhood in so many ways.

The Hough Riots 1966 Brought a Big Change in the City of Cleveland

Carl B. Stokes African American was elected the 51stMayor of Cleveland, Ohio

On November 7, 1967 and took office on January 1, 1968. He was instrumental in helping to calm down the ripple effects of the 1966 Hough Riots and Glenville Riots.

Senator Robert F. Kennedy was assassinated in June 1968

The Music of the 1960;s helped many families to deal with the 1960s with the triumph, tragedies of families and assassination of three great world leaders President John F. Kennedy, Dr. Martin L. King Jr. and Senator Robert F. Kennedy.

Music of the sixties and many more. This is just few of the favorite among family members listen around the 1966 Hough Riots and after. The music of the 1960's helped many families with all traumata going on in the community and all around the world. It helped sooth our minds and relaxed the body by dancing to the music.

Aretha Franklin	**Respect**
B. B. King	**The Thrill Is Gone**
Beatles	**A Hard Day's Night**
James Brown	**I Got You (I Feel Good)**
Contours	**Do You Love Me**
Stevie Wonder	**Fingertips**
The Supremes	**Stop! In The Name of Love**

What We Had and What We Lost

What We Had

Our Family

Barber Shops

Bakery

Cleveland Public Schools

Cleveland Public Libraries

Community Leaders

Communication

City of Cleveland

Churches

Cleveland Support Staff

Dry Cleaners

Drug Store

Homes

League Recreation Center

Mount Sinai Hospital

Record Shop

Supermarkets

What We Lost

Respect to ourselves

Bakeries

Barber Shops

Communications-Positive

Collaborations

Community Leaders

Dry Cleaners

Drug Store

Homes

Long Time Residents

Long Time Property Owners

LongTime Establishments

Record shop

Restaurants

Supermarkets

**The 1966 Hough Riots
Encourage Me to Listen and Learn**

Bobbie Brooks

Cleveland, Ohio

First employment sewing position: After graduating from East High School, I applied for employment sewing position with Bobbie Books women clothing store located at plant 2230 Superior Avenue. I was hired and accepted the position. I was assigned to sew pieces for teenager girl dresses. After, a few months I did not like the environment of the atmosphere and attitudes of my supervisors.

During that time, I decided to apply for employment with The Richmond Brothers Company. They hired me to work at their sewing plant and I gave Bobbie Brooks one week notice. I went directly there to become an employee with The Richmond Brothers Company.

The Richmond Brothers Company

Cleveland, Ohio

Second employment sewing position: The Richmond Brothers Company was founded in 1853 by Jewish-Bavarian newcomers Richmond and Lehman Family. In 1879 the business was moved to a challenging city, Cleveland, Ohio to enlarge their operations to their consumers. The factory location was very visible on 55th street. It was a very spacious building with large front windows.

I applied for the sewing position with The Richmond Brothers Company and accepted the position for piece work assignment sewing individual pieces for men suits. I enjoyed my experiences working in a sewing factory and learning techniques of putting a men suit jacket together.

The staff at the Richmond Brothers were nice and patient with me and the atmosphere was pleasant to work in. The supervisor's name was Axel one of the nicest persons you could ever meet. He trained me how to sew more efficiently with my piece work assignments, which helped to increase my income. However, this was not the employment I wanted for my career, but it was a start.

The Day Nursery Association

Cleveland, Ohio

I wanted to become a preschool teacher. Lucky, one day my mind directed me to contact The Day Nursery Association by telephone and spoked to Mrs. Utz director of personnel. I asked if they were hiring for preschool teacher assistant, and she said "no" "I will send you an application."

She did send me an application in the mail, and I was so excited about my dream was about to happen. I was nervously opening the envelope and gazed over the application. Anxiously ready to fill out the application and my mom assisted me in completing the application and I immediately sent it back.

Then about two weeks I received a telephone call from Mrs. Utz. She asked me "Ms. Graffenreed are you still interested in teacher assistant position with our organization" I" said "yes." An interview was set up for me that next week.

I went to the interview at The Day Nursery Association main office located at2084 Cornell Road in University Circle near Case Western Reserve University. I remembered wearing a white blouse, blue skirt, black pumps, my mom's beautiful pin, pearl necklace and clip on earrings.

I planned not to be shy because this is the career I truly wanted to pursue in life. I was nervous, delighted and feeling blessed for the opportunity. I was ready for the challenge, Aunt Katie and mom talked to me about staying focus, looking the interview in the eyes, listening, answer questions and being sincere if I really wanted to become a preschool teacher assistant.

The first interview went well. The second part of the interview a scheduled morning interview was arranged to go to Lakeview Terrace Child Care Center. Located in the Metropolitan Housing Estate Community Center located on near westside.

I was feeling nervous about going to the westside of Cleveland. I rode the Public Transportation from the eastside Hough Avenue to the near westside 25th street. I walked along ways down a hill and under a bridge toward the lake. I was

determined to find the Lakeview Terrace Child Care Center and I did. I was punctual and appreciating the opportunity.

Once I met the Director Mrs. Bracy she welcomed me with open arms and the most beautiful smile and attitude. I was introduced to the staff and children. The preschool was clean and organized and the children were playing.

I observed the teachers seem like they were enjoying playing with the children and interacting with parents as they were bringing their children to school. They greeted the children and parents with a warm welcoming smile and saying "Good Morning" greeting the children and parents by name.

I felt very relaxed and incredibly lucky because my dream is becoming reality. I stayed for a half a day as requested to observe the routine on how teachers interact with the children, and I did. The experience was impressing and rewarding. The Director Mrs. Bracy stated: how please she was how I interacted with the children and staff. She recommended me to be hired. I accepted the position and that was one of my happiest days of my life. I was on my way to pursue my dream becoming a preschool teacher assistant.

My dream became true/reality because three women Personnel Director (Caucasian) Mrs. Utz, Director(Caucasian) Mrs. Haffey and Preschool Director (African American) Mrs. Bracy believed in me!

Mrs. Bracy was a mother to her young staff. She would talk to us about work ethics. How to demonstrate professionalism in the work environment. At Lakeview Terrace Child Care Center, we always have had visitors from the primary office and out of town.

Mr. & Mrs. James Haynes, Mrs. Bracy and mom encourage me to enroll in Cuyahoga Community College to pursue my education in Early Childhood Education. When I received my first evaluation from Mrs. Bracy, and it was favorable and fair. She was pleased with my attendance, my attitude toward the children, parents, and staff. I demonstrated my interest in working with young children and their parents. She can see the potential in me and would like me to enroll in one class in Early Childhood Education 101 at Cuyahoga Community College. She released me from work in the mornings two days a week with pay. She would go into the classroom in my absence while I was in class and encouraged me to retain my first textbook in 101 Early Childhood Education " The Years Before School". By Todd and Heffernan and start Early Childhood Library at home. I did and we are still friends today and communicate with one another.

University Towers

Cleveland, Ohio
Located in the Hough Community

University Towers was one the first rental properties we stayed in before locating to Orange County, California. So, I could pursue a preschool teacher position in the Orange County Head Start Program in Santa Ana, California. It was such a wonderful experience meeting and interacting with longtime Californians.

Although, I lived 3,000 miles away from (Hometown) Cleveland, Ohio. The experiences with growing up in the Hough neighborhood with family, friends, Cleveland Public Schools, Cuyahoga Community College, Bobbie Brooks, The Richmond Brothers and The Day Nursery Association prepared me for the real world.

Mount Sinai Hospital

Cleveland, Ohio

The Mount Sinai Hospital was established and grew out of the work of Young Ladies of Hebrew in early days in 1882 for Jewish doctors. Who were not permitted to practice in other hospitals in the City of Cleveland. During those times because of aggressive behaviors actions toward Jewish people.

Mount Sinai Hospital began their journey in latter part of 1800's on East 32nd street and moved into place/building in the Hough Community on 105th Street in early 1900s. The hospital was not only a Jewish Hospital but for underprivileged community as well as around the 1950's.

During the years Mount Sinai Hospital served the Hough Community and other communities quite well. They *were known for not turning anyone away.* The residents who lived in the community had the opportunity to become employees and walked to the hospital if needed.

On July 18, 1966 on sizzling summer night around 8:30 pm the Hough Riots broke out on 79th Hough Avenue. Mount Sinai Hospital was nearby to care for the wounded and trauma effects of the riots. The administrators and their staff provided excellent care/performance for the injured victims of the riots.

Appreciation

Longtime ago, my grandmother and mom were a patient at Mount Sinai Hospital. They both passed away in the hospital and received excellent care especially during their dying days.

My mom loved Mount Sinai Hospital. She has been a client for many years and felt comfortable with her primary doctor. When her doctor was out of town. She only scheduled her appointments. When her doctor would be presence.

When my mom became gravely ill. The physician stated to the family :" Looking at your mother's medical chart" "she has had nine lives" "but this illness that is going to take out" we decided to stay in the (hospital in shifts with our mom while she was dying).

The grandchildren in mornings, brother and sister in evening and me (GWEN) stayed during the nights. Since I stayed during the night, a bed was provided for me next to my mom. While the physician would examine my mom I was examine as well as for seven nights until she passed away.

During those times and moments physician, nurses, and supportive staff was so nice to me. Always wanted to accommodate me asking would I like something to eat or drink. I would also reply by saying "no, thank you" . My mom passed away peacefully with the excellent care from Mount Sinai Hospital team.

I will always be grateful to Mount Sinai Hospital for the service they provided for my family and the families of the Hough community. Gwen Graffenreed

A Doctor's Reflections On Mt. Sinai Hospital

I am currently a practicing orthopedic surgeon whose career began at Mount Sinai Hospital back in 1980. It is at Mount Sinai Hospital where I first met my wife, and I began my journey into medicine. I have nothing but fond memories of the time that I spent at Mount Sinai Hospital. In 1980 as a medical student, I began my introduction into the healthcare system and was most impressed by the caring relationship of the hospital system to the surrounding local community. Spending my next five years as an orthopedic resident at Mount Sinai I got to be part of that system by helping to run the orthopedic clinic and I not only was able to service the people in the immediate area, but I also learned what it really meant to be a doctor.

After finishing my residency, I spent 2 years of fellowship training away from Cleveland. During this time, I did some advanced training in total joint replacement and sports medicine. In 1989 I returned to Cleveland to Mount Sinai Hospital where I open my practice. I not only returned to taking care of people in the local community, but I also brought people from eastern suburbs to Mount Sinai Hospital to receive their orthopedic specialty care.

It should be mentioned that at that time. Mount Sinai Hospital had the opportunity to leave the local community and move out into eastern suburbs. Instead, they chose not to move and put all their resources into the existing hospital thereby showing a true dedication to the neighborhood.

Unfortunately, due to the changing landscape of the healthcare system Mount Sinai Hospital closed its doors in 2000. Despite closing the doors their presence is still felt throughout Greater Cleveland and its suburbs through the doctors who trained and practice there. I am proud to be one of those doctors and thank you Mount Sinai for all you have done for me.

Bruce T. Cohn, M.D.
Orthopedic Surgeon

Crises in the United States of America

I was fascinated with a quote by President John F. Kennedy

"As not what your country can do for you"" Ask what you can do for your country." JFK

Dr. Martin L. King Jr. was a great leader for the for Non-violent approach.

Senator Robert F. Kennedy predicted in one of his quotes. "The Irish was not wanted there" (When his grandfather came to Boston) " Now Irish Catholic is the President of the United States of America" "there is no questions about it" "In the next forty years a Negro can achieve the same position that my brother has" RFK.

His prediction became true within the forty years, Barrack Obama was elected in 2009. To become the forty-fourth President of the United States of America.

The three Great Crusaders was President John F. Kennedy, Dr. Martin L. King Jr., and Senator Robert F. Kennedy. They were assassinated because of their strong dedication and strong faith in their mission. Once it was completed. It was time for them to go and they did. However, they will be remembered in the history books for their courage, inspiring justice for all human beings in United States of America.

Many residents on Lexington Avenue did not approve of the Hough Riots. We had great leaders during the 1960's all over the world. Growing up during a period of challenging times will make you or break you . If you allowed this to happen. Many of us steadily adjusted being appreciative what we did have.

Transportation

Living In Cleveland, Ohio Without Vehicle

In 1960's living in the Hough community "some families did not own a vehicle. Only transportation they had was riding The Greater regional Transit Authority bus (RTA).

Local Buses RTA bus system brings extensive service throughout the City of Cleveland and other Cuyahoga County Communities.

Express and Flyer Buses brings longer distant less stops usually connecting Cleveland's suburbs with downtown.

Rapid Rail faster way to travel to your destination.

Bicycling in the Cleveland area is excellent way for getting around.

Until this day many families do not own vehicles and depends on Public Transportation. Let us ask the question. Could you live in Cleveland, Ohio without a vehicle ? "You might say "NO" I am here to say YES if you had too." To decide to buy a house or vehicle What would you do? *PLANNING IS THE ANSWER* .

Hough Neighborhood

Has Been Historically Residential Community

Overall, The Hough Neighborhood on The Famous Lexington Avenue where I lived fifty years ago is steadily progressing.

The former The League Park Community Center is now The Baseball Heritage Museum located on Lexington Avenue in the Hough neighborhood.

I had the opportunity to visit Hough Neighborhood where I grew up on Lexington Avenue. Fatima Family Center. On Saturday July 12, 2022 as a Board member with The Legal Aid Society of Cleveland for Community Legal Aid Clinic. It was such a rewarding day seeing the residents coming in and learning about the Legal services that is provided for the community.

On Saturday November 12, 2023 I was invited to attend Cleveland Public Library New Branch Hough Library Ribbon Cutting Ceremony. I was so delighted to be invited and I enjoyed myself with the many other quest that were there. Just being around the neighborhood and seeing all the upgrading that is going on with buildings and the homes and apartment buildings.

Catholic Charities their Fatima Family Center is serving the families and children in a variety of ways. They have a Senior Center Program which is very much needed.

Going into the neighborhood I grew up on Lexington Avenue many years ago brought such good feelings. I made it because so many people believed in me beside my family.

The Art of Letter Writing

In the early days letter writing is one of the ways people would communicate with their families and friends. It is nice to receive a handwritten letter once and awhile. It allows you to read it repeatedly. Writing is a gift that I believe gives you time to think, to communicate, to organize and to express your feelings to become more relax in our own skin.

During the nineteen sixties my mom would write short letters to family members who lived out of town. I was so fascinated just watching her ink pen go up and down as she was writing. Once she completed writing the letter. She would address the envelope. Then it was time to put the letter inside the envelope and seal it and placing a stamp up on right upper corner of the envelope. Then the letter is ready to be mailed.

St. Louis, Mo., 10 - 4 - 19 47

7   Form 55—5M—8-47

THIS IS TO CERTIFY that the Precinct Registers of
WARD 4 PRECINCT 29
of the City of St. Louis, State of Missouri, contain the following
Registration:

Name REED WILL HENRY.
(Last Name)   (First Name)   (Middle Name)

1673 CORINTH AVE
(House Number)   (Street)

Date of application for Registration 10 - 22 - 47

Registration cancelled

Date of Birth 2 - 2 - 15 Place Mississippi

BOARD OF ELECTION COMMISSIONERS
FOR THE CITY OF ST. LOUIS

Frank L. Ramacciotti, Chairman   Wm. J. Studt, Member
Lawrence Boogher, Member   H. A. Hamilton, Member
                                                        and Secretary

This is NOT a certificate which
in any way entitles a person to
vote, and shall NOT prevent or   By
discourage a challenge at the
polls.   CHIEF CLERK.

In the 1960's Great Maternal Uncle Will Reed sent a copy of his 1947

Voter Registration form. To my mom Rebecca to encourage her to register to vote.

FAMILY PHOTOS

Maternal Sisters

Aunt Katherine

My Mom Rebecca

Gwen Graffenreed

References

Call and Post Newspaper

Case Western Reserve University Encyclopedia of Cleveland History

Cleveland Public Library

Cleveland Public Schools

Cleveland State University

County Library

Ebony Magazine

Jet Magazine

Plain Dealer Newspaper

The City of Cleveland

Wikipedia

Printed in the United States
by Baker & Taylor Publisher Services